Is Afrikan Spirituality A Religion
By Blak Pantha

© Kofi Piesie ReSearch Team. © Same Tree Different Branch

Kofi Piesie/Mossi Warrior Clan
Copyright 2020 by Kofi Piesie Research Team

All rights reserved. No part of this book may be reproduced or transmitted in any form or by any means, electronic or mechanical, including photocopying, recording, or by any information storage and retrieval systems without the written permission of the publisher.

Printed in the United States of America

Table of Contents

Forward	6
Majority Religion by Country	7
Size of Major Religious Groups	8
The Definition of Religion More or Less	9
What is Folk Religion	11
What Are They Saying by Folk Religion	13
Christianity	15
Islam	17
Judaism	19
Buddhism	21
Hindusim	23
Zoroastrianism	25
Volume of Sacred Law	29
Working Definition of Religion	30
The Question Must Be Asked	31
What is Afrikan Spirituality	32

Religious Categories	**33**
Animism	**35**
Animism Analysis	**37**
Monotheism	**39**
Monotheism Analysis	**41**
Polytheism	**43**
Polytheism Analysis	**45**
Panentheism	**47**
Panentheism Analysis	**49**
Pantheism	**51**
Pantheism Analysis	**53**
Neoplatonism	**55**
Neoplatonism Analysis	**57**
Henotheism	**59**
Henotheism Analysis	**61**
Monolatrism	**63**
Monolatrism Analysis	**65**
Kathenotheism	**67**
Kathenotheism Analyst	**69**

Lets Look At some Afrikan Systems 71

Dogon 73

A Fat Roog 75

Mbuti 77

Ngoma 79

Mossi 81

Odinani/Omenala 83

Ìṣẹ̀ṣe Làgbà 85

Ki.môyo 87

References 88

Forward

The first thing you should know about this book is that it started as a presentation in 2019. I initially put together that presentation to highlight the differences between Afrikan spirituality and religion. I discovered the scholastic categorization of religions when putting that presentation together. I quickly noticed that after I put out that presentation, the topic was sidestepped or flat-out ignored by contemporaries and colleagues.

Though no one challenged my findings, there was also not much acknowledgment in works that followed that centered on the same topic. I always think it's not good enough to be correct and that it's better to be effective. I expanded on the subject from my presentation and created a book to illustrate my position in this argument further. I sincerely hope you enjoy the read, and I hope to be more effective with this current analysis.

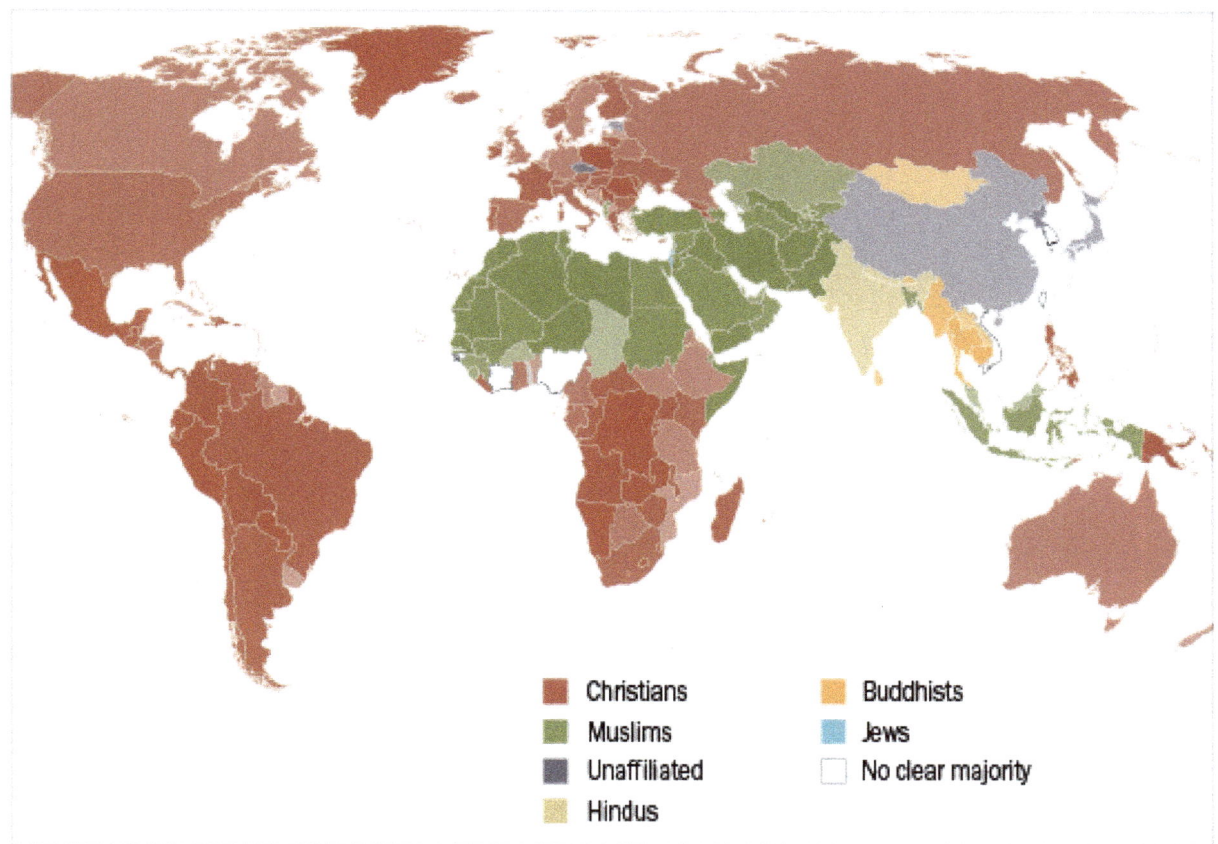

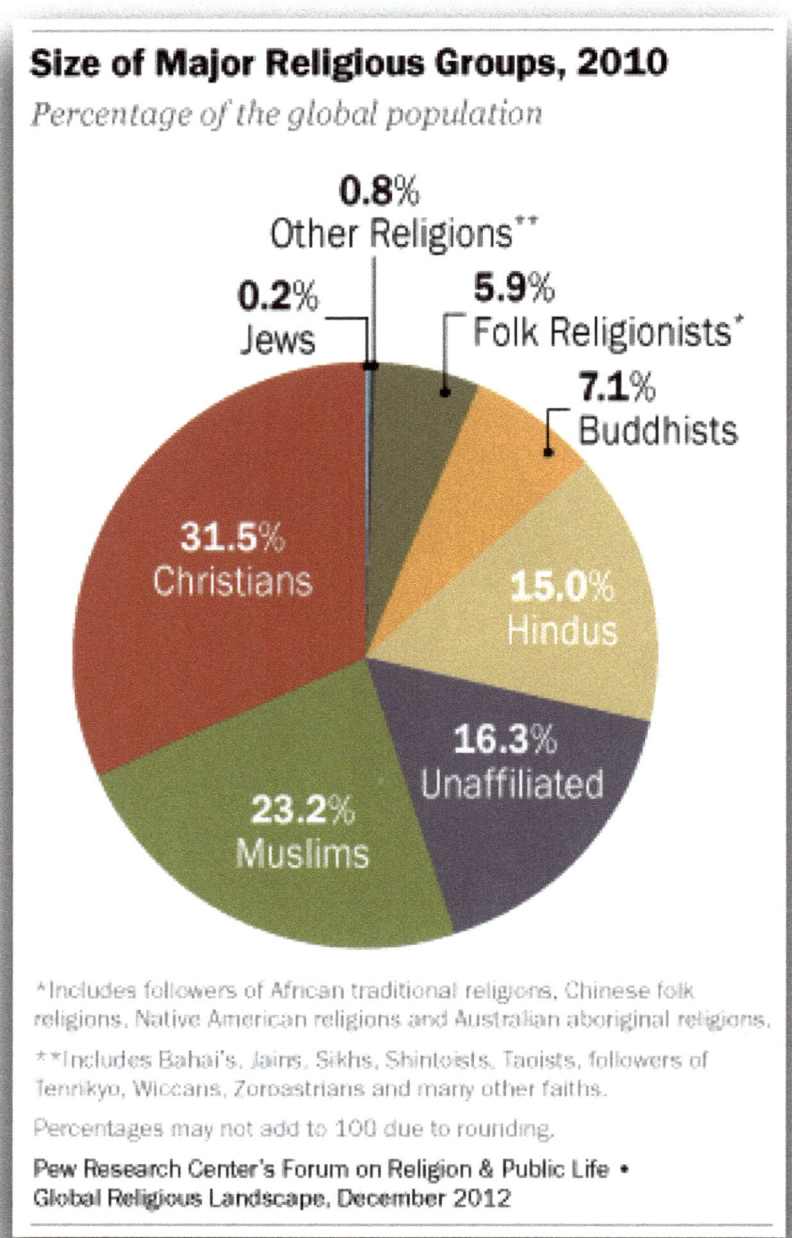

The Definition of Religion More or Less

Religion may be defined as a cultural system of designated behaviors and practices, worldviews, texts, sanctified places, prophecies, ethics, or organizations that relate humanity to supernatural, transcendental, or spiritual elements. However, there is no scholarly consensus over what precisely constitutes a religion. Scholars have disagreed on a definition of religion. There are two general definition systems: the sociological/functional and the phenomenological/philosophical religion is a modern Western concept. Similar concepts are not found in many current and past cultures; there is no equivalent term for religion in many languages. Scholars have found it challenging to develop a consistent definition, with some giving up on the possibility of a definition. Others argue that applying it to non-Western cultures is inappropriate regardless of its meaning.

The MacMillan Encyclopedia of Religions states the very attempt to define religion, to find some distinctive or possibly unique essence or set of qualities that distinguish the religious from the remainder of human life, is primarily a Western concern. The attempt is a natural consequence of the Western speculative, intellectualistic, and scientific disposition. It is also the product of the dominant Western religious mode, the Judeo-Christian climate, or, more accurately, the theistic inheritance from Judaism, Christianity, and Islam. The theistic form of belief in this tradition, even when downgraded culturally, is formative of the dichotomous Western view of religion. The basic structure of theism is essentially a distinction between a transcendent deity and all else, between the creator and his creation, and between God and man. There are an estimated 10,000 distinct religions worldwide. Still, about 84% of the world's population is affiliated with one of the five largest religion groups, namely Christianity, Islam, Hinduism, Buddhism, or forms of folk religion. If you notice, the so-called African religions are labeled as Folk religions.

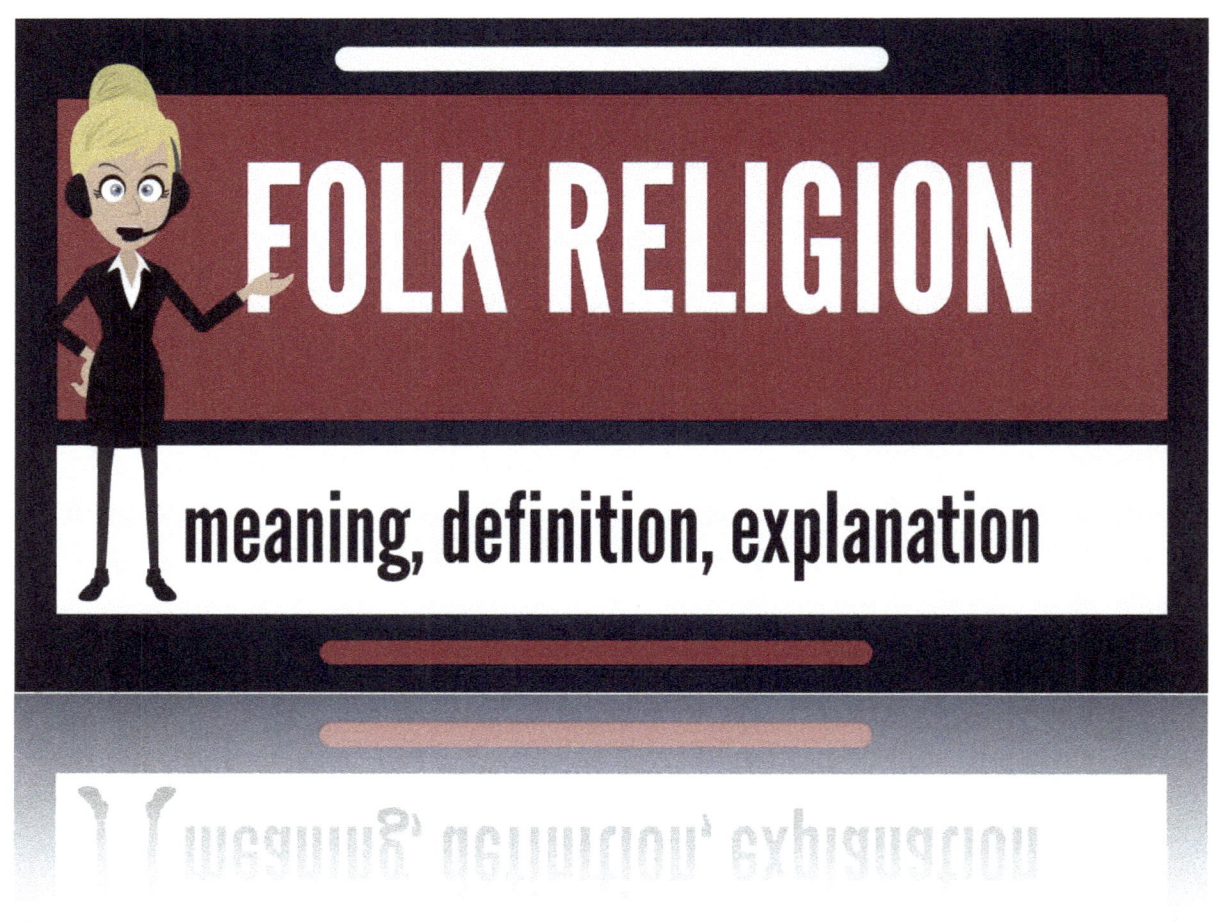

What is Folk Religion

In religious studies and folkloristics, **folk religion**, **popular religion**, or **vernacular religion** comprises various forms and expressions of religion distinct from the official doctrines and practices of organized religion. The precise definition of folk religion varies among scholars. Sometimes also termed **popular belief**, it consists of ethnic or regional religious customs under the umbrella of religion but outside official doctrine and practices.

Folk Christianity is defined differently by various scholars. Definitions include "the Christianity practiced by a conquered people," Christianity as most people live it is a term used to "overcome the division of beliefs into Orthodox and unorthodox," Christianity as impacted by superstition as practiced by certain geographical Christian groups, and Christianity defined "in cultural terms without reference to the theologies and histories. Folk Islam is an umbrella term used to collectively describe forms of Islam that incorporate native folk beliefs and practices.

Folk Islam has been described as the Islam of the "urban poor, country people, and tribes" in contrast to orthodox or "High" Islam (Gellner, 1992). Sufism and Sufi concepts are often integrated into Folk Islam.

Folk Judaism defined Jewish folk religion as consisting of ideas and practices that, while not meeting with the approval of religious leaders, enjoyed wide popularity such that they must be included in what he termed the field of religion.

What Are They Saying by Folk Religion?

The question must be asked. What are these religious scholars saying by calling Afrikan spiritual practices folk religions? This folk religion designation is a political move that projects power and bias amongst multiple types of worshippers globally. Essentially, they have created an unofficial hierarchy that includes Afrikan spirituality but places them at the bottom. They have recognized our practices as religions but identified them as unofficial and unapproved versions of the three dominant monotheistic religions. Remember, folk religion is synonymous with urban, poor, unapproved, low, unofficial, etc. So, the religions that came after the Afrikan spiritual practices called the indigenous practices these terms and placed their practices above those they disapproved of. Make no mistake that this is white supremacy in action. Whenever we refer to our spiritual traditions as African Traditional Religions or ATR or anything that encompasses the religion term, we support white supremacy and its racist designation of our practices. I realize scholars like John Mbiti fought hard for our practices to be recognized as legitimate religions. Still, I doubt he wanted us to be disrespected and placed at the bottom rather than on equal footing with every other practice. Let's now look at some religions that aren't categorized as folk so we can be familiar with some key components of their framework.

Christianity

Christianity is an Abrahamic monotheistic religious group based on the life and teachings of Jesus of Nazareth, also known by Christians as Christ. Its adherents believe that Jesus is the Son of God, the Logos, and the savior of humanity, whose coming as the Messiah (Christ) was prophesied in the Old prominent role in shaping Western civilization. Christianity and its ethics have played a significant role in shaping Western culture.

The main points include:
- Belief in God the Father, Jesus Christ as the Son of God, and the Holy Spirit
- The death, descent into hell, resurrection, and ascension of Christ

- The holiness of the Church and the communion of saints

- Christ's second coming, the Day of Judgement, and salvation of the faithful.

Islam

Islam is an Abrahamic monotheistic religion teaching that there is only one God (Allah and that Muhammad is the messenger of God Islam teaches that God is merciful, all-powerful, and unique and has guided humanity through prophets, revealed scriptures, and natural signs. The primary scriptures of Islam are the Quran, viewed by Muslims as the verbatim word of God, and the teachings and normative example (called the *sunnah*, composed of accounts called *hadith*) of Muhammad (c. 570–8 June 632 CE). Muslims consider the Quran to be the unaltered and final revelation of God. Like other Abrahamic religions, Islam also teaches a final judgment with the righteous rewarded in paradise and the unrighteous punished in hell. Religious concepts and practices include the Five Pillars of Islam, which are obligatory acts of worship, and following Islamic law (*sharia*), which touches on virtually every aspect of life and society, from banking and welfare to women and the environment. The cities of Mecca, Medina, and Jerusalem are home to the three holiest sites in Islam.

Judaism

Judaism is the religion of the Jewish people. It is an ancient, monotheistic, Abrahamic religion with the Torah as its foundational text. It encompasses the religion, philosophy, and culture of the Jewish people. Religious Jews consider Judaism to be the expression of the covenant god established with the Children of Israel. Judaism encompasses a vast corpus of texts, practices, theological positions, and forms of organization. The Torah is part of the larger text known as the Tanakh or the Hebrew Bible, and supplemental oral tradition is represented by later texts such as the Midrash and the Talmud. With between 14.5 and 17.4 million adherents worldwide.

20

Buddhism

Buddhism An Indian religion, Buddhism encompasses a variety of traditions, beliefs, and spiritual practices primarily based on original teachings attributed to the Buddha and resulting interpreted philosophies. Buddhism originated in Ancient India as a Sramana tradition sometime between the 6th and 4th centuries BCE, spreading through much of Asia. Scholars generally recognize two major extant branches of Buddhism: Theravada (Pali: "The School of the Elders") and Mahayana (Sanskrit: "The Great Vehicle"). All Buddhist traditions share the goal of overcoming suffering and the cycle of death & rebirth, either by attaining Nirvana or through the path of Buddhahood. Buddhist schools vary in their interpretation of the path to liberation, the relative importance and canonicity assigned to the various Buddhist texts, and their specific teachings and practices. Widely observed methods include taking refuge in the Buddha, the Dharma, and the Sangha, observing moral precepts, monasticism, meditation, and cultivating the Paramitas (virtues). Buddhist texts were initially passed on orally by monks. Still, they were later written down and composed as manuscripts in various Indo-Aryan languages, which were then translated into other local languages as Buddhism spread. Vinaya, Sutra, and the Abhidharma.

Hinduism

Hinduism is an Indian religion and *dharma*, or a way of life, widely practiced in the Indian subcontinent. Hinduism has been called the oldest religion in the world, and some practitioners and scholars refer to it as *Sanātana Dharma*, "the eternal tradition," or the "eternal way," beyond human history. Scholars regard Hinduism as a fusion or synthesis [of various Indian cultures and traditions, with diverse roots and no founder. This "Hindu synthesis" developed between 500 BCE and 300 CE, following the Vedic period (1500 BCE to 500 BCE). Although Hinduism contains a broad range of philosophies, it is linked by shared concepts, recognizable rituals, cosmology, shared textual resources, and pilgrimage to sacred sites. Hindu texts are classified into Śruti ("heard") and Smṛti ("remembered"). These texts discuss theology, philosophy, mythology, Vedic yajna, Yoga, agamic rituals, and temple building, among other topics. Primary scriptures include the Vedas and Upanishads, the *Bhagavad Gita*, and the Agamas. Sources of authority and eternal truths in its texts play an important role. Still, there is also a strong Hindu tradition of questioning authority to deepen understanding of these truths and further develop its practice.

Zoroastrianism

Zoroastrianism, or **Mazdayasna**, is one of the world's oldest religions that remains active. It is a monotheistic faith (i.e., a single creator god) centered in a dualistic cosmology of good and evil and an eschatology predicting the ultimate destruction of evil. Ascribed to the teachings of the Iranian-speaking prophet Zoroaster (also known as Zarathustra), it exalts a deity of wisdom, Ahura Mazda (*Wise Lord*), as its Supreme Being. Major features of Zoroastrianism, such as messianism, judgment after death, heaven and hell, and free will, have influenced other religious systems, including Second Temple Judaism, Gnosticism, Christianity, and Islam.

The most important texts of the religion are those of the *Avesta*, which includes the writings of Zoroaster known as the Gathas, enigmatic poems that define the religion's precepts, and the Yasna, the scripture. The full name by which Zoroaster addressed the deity is Ahura, The Lord Creator, and Mazda, Supremely Wise. The religious philosophy of Zoroaster divided the early Iranian gods of Proto-Indo-Iranian tradition but focused on responsibility and did not create a devil per-se. Zoroaster proclaimed that there is only one God, the singularly creative and sustaining force of the Universe and that human beings are given a right of choice.

Because of cause and effect, they are responsible for the consequences of their choices. Tngra Mainyu, or angry spirit., was the contesting force to Ahura Mazda Post-Zoroastrian scripture introduced the concept of Ahriman, the devil, which was effectively a personification of Angra Mainyu. In Zoroastrianism, the purpose in life is to "be among those who renew the world...to make the world progress towards perfection".

Its fundamental maxims include:

- Humata, Hukhta, Huvarshta, which means: Good Thoughts, Good Words, Good Deeds.

- There is only one path, and that is the path of Truth.

- Do the right thing because it is the right thing to do, and then all beneficial rewards will come to you also.

VSL: A Main Component in Religion

The Volume of Sacred Law (VSL) (also known as the **Book of the Law**) is the Masonic term for whatever religious or philosophical texts are displayed during a Lodge meeting. VSL teaches us:
- the all-important duties we owe to God, our neighbors, and ourselves.

- It is to be regarded as the unerring standard of Truth and Justice.

- It teaches us to believe in the wise dispensation of Divine Providence.

- It is to rule and govern our faith.

This tool is a significant component and many times a requirement in religions

Working Definition of Religion

Religion is a modern, primarily western concept and cultural belief system that encompasses a belief in a higher power and has a dependence on a volume of sacred law to instruct its believers on morality and faith. Not centered around testing and proving.

The questions must be asked:

What is Afrikan spirituality?

If Afrikan spirituality is indeed a religion, what religious category does it fall under?

We will look through a few of these categories to see if Afrikan people's spiritual framework fits within numerous religions that are standard in religious academia.

What is Afrikan Spirituality?

Afrikan Spirituality – the commonalities of the indigenous systems of Afrikans across the continent whose goal is too manifest energies, worship natural forces in the Universe, and venerate progenitors and ancestors.

Religious Categories

- **Animism**

- **Monotheism**

- **Polytheism**

- **Panentheism**

- **Pantheism**

- **Neoplatonism**

- **Henotheism**

- **Monolatrism**

- **Katheontheism**

E. B. Tylor. Aet. 67
From a photograph by Hault and Fox

Animism

Animism is the religious belief that objects, places, and creatures possess a distinct spiritual essence. Potentially, animism perceives all things animals, plants, rocks, rivers, weather systems, human handiwork, and perhaps even words as animated and alive.

Animism is the world's oldest religion, "Animism predates any form of organized religion and is said to contain the oldest spiritual and supernatural perspective in the world. It dates to the Paleolithic Age, when humans roamed the plains, hunting, gathering, and communing with the Spirit of Nature. Whether animism refers to an ancestral mode of experience common to indigenous peoples worldwide or a full-fledged religion in its own right, the currently accepted definition of animism was only developed in the late 19th century (1871) by Sir Edward Tyler, who created it as "one of anthropology's earliest concepts, if not The idea of animism was developed by the anthropologist Sir Edward Tyler in his 1871 book *Primitive Culture*, in which he defined it as "the general doctrine of souls and other spiritual beings in general."

According to Tyler, animism often includes "an idea of pervading life and will in nature"; a belief that natural objects other than humans have souls.

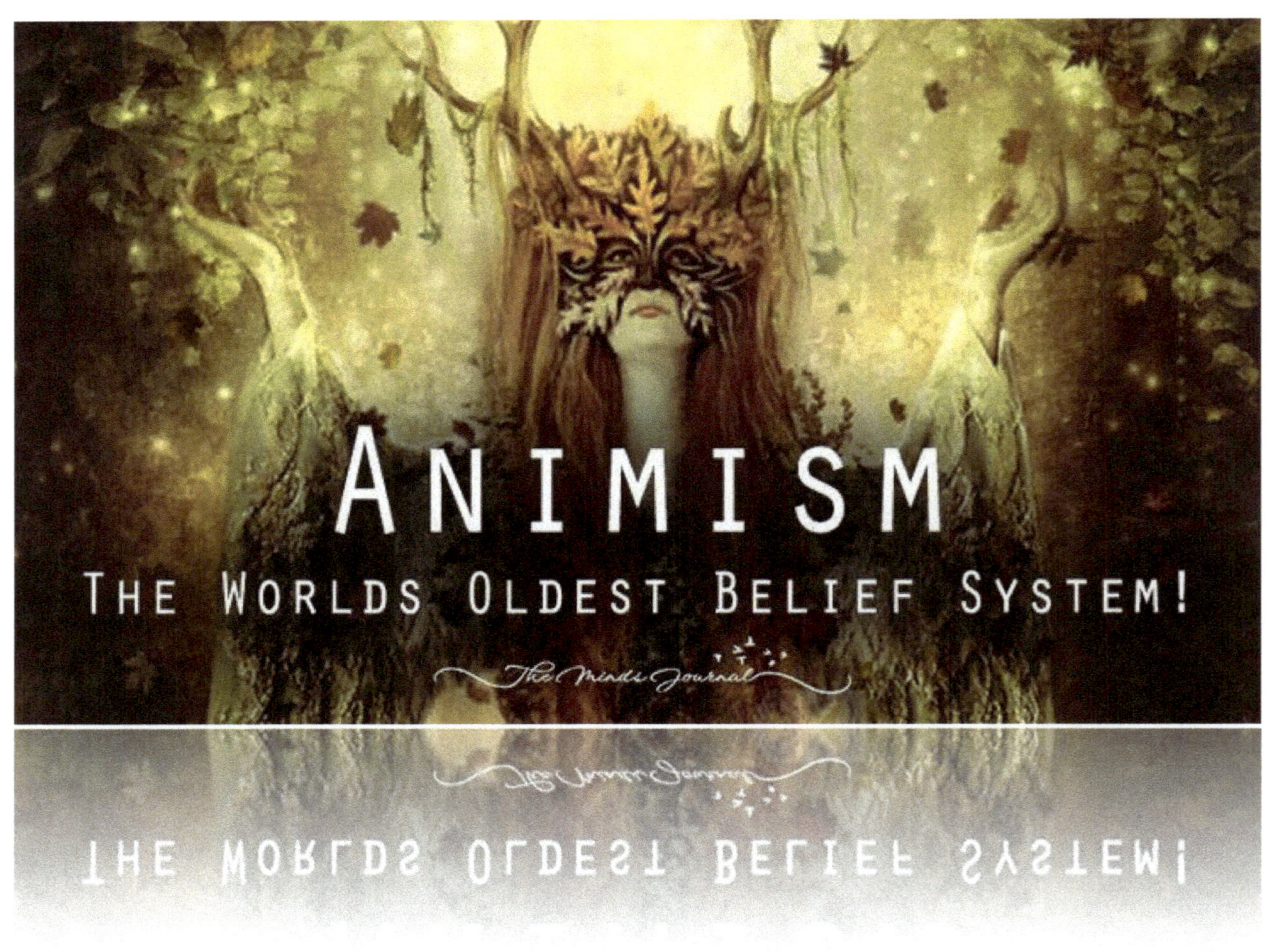

Animism Analysis

I must admit Edward Tyler's analysis of Animism is very close to the Afrikan spiritual framework found on the continent. Animism comes from the Latin word anima, which means breath or life. We cannot use Animism as a religious designator from Afrikan Spirituality because Edward Tyler's text mentions animism in his book Primitive Culture. This is where he shows his bias towards Afrikan people by calling their culture primitive. When relating to people, the word primitive becomes an offensive term meaning unsophisticated, underdeveloped, low, crude, and not evolved. This is his perspective, placing his way of life above the Afrikan way of life. He sees his way of life as superior to ours. We are teetering on racism now. Theoretically, Afrikan people cannot see Animism as a spiritual epithet due to its racial undertones.

Monotheism

Monotheism has been defined as the belief in the existence of only one God that created the world, is all-powerful, and intervenes in the world. A broader definition of monotheism is the belief in one God The more expansive definition of monotheism characterizes the traditions of Bábism, the Bahá'í Faith, Balinese Hinduism, Cao Dai (Caodaism), Cheondoism (Cheondogyo), Christianity, Deism, Eckankar, Hindu sects such as Shaivism and Vaishnavism, Islam, Judaism, Mandaeism, Rastafari, Seicho no Ie, Sikhism, Tengrism (Tangrism), Tenrikyo (Tenriism), Yazidism, and Zoroastrianism, and elements of pre-monotheistic thought are found in early religions such as ancient Chinese religion, and Yahwism.

Monotheism Analysis

Monotheism has never been in the Afrikan traditional spiritual framework. Yes, Afrikan has creator deities, but in the collective of what we call Afrikan spirituality, a key concept debunks Afrikan being monotheist. Creator deities have little to no interaction with Afrikan people. In fact, this is one of the reasons we have lesser deities like Òrìṣà, Never, Abossom, Lwa, Etc.

There is a Yoruba Story of Olódùmarè sitting up in the heavens, holding back the rain due to the misbehavior of other Òrìṣà. Rather than eliminate them, he watched them learn from their mistakes and suffer in the drought. The Òrìṣà suffered until they begged for forgiveness, but Olódùmarè could not hear because he was too high in the heavens. Òrìṣà could not reach where he was. Let's think about this logically. Òrìṣà are Olódùmarè divine creations.

They are deities themselves, and Olódùmarè was so far away he could not even hear their cries. So, as humans or eniyan (Chosen ones in the Yoruba language), you can imagine the access we have to the supreme deity and his interaction with us is slim to none.

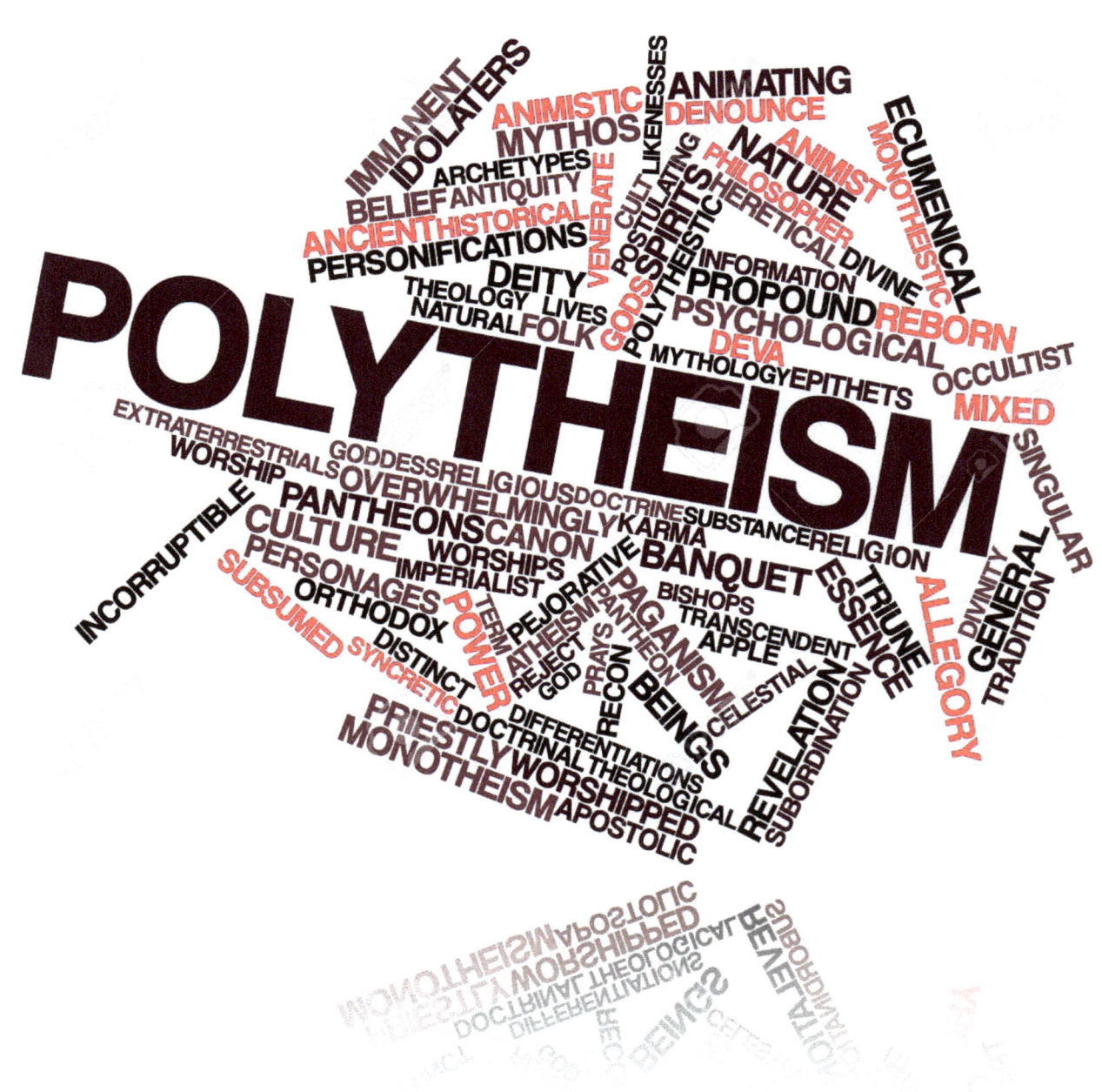

Polytheism

Polytheism (from Greek πολυθεϊσμός, *polytheisms)* is the worship of or belief in multiple deities, which are usually assembled into a pantheon of gods and goddesses, along with their religions and rituals. In most religions that accept polytheism, the different gods and goddesses are representations of forces of nature or ancestral principles. They can be viewed either as autonomous or as aspects or emanations of a creator deity or absolute transcendental principle (monistic theologies), manifesting immanently in nature (panentheistic and pantheistic religions).

Polytheism is a type of theism. Within theism, it contrasts with monotheism, the belief in a singular God, in most cases transcendent. Polytheists do not always worship all the gods equally, but they can be henotheists, specializing in worshiping one particular deity. Other polytheists can be kathenotheists, worshiping different deities at different times. "Hard" polytheism believes that gods are distinct, separate, real divine beings rather than psychological archetypes or personifications of natural forces. Hard polytheists reject the idea that" all gods are one God" "Hard" polytheists do not necessarily consider the gods of all cultures equally authentic, a theological position formally known as integrational polytheism or omnism.

This is contrasted with "soft" polytheism, which holds that gods may be aspects of only one God and that the pantheons of other cultures are representative of one single pantheon, psychological archetypes, or personifications of natural forces.

Polytheism Analysis

Since polytheism is the belief that gods are distinct, separate, real divine beings rather than psychological archetypes or personifications of natural forces, it contrasts with Afrikan cultural phenomena. Afrikan has many deities that are the personification of natural forces, but they also see these entities as real deities.

Depending on the spiritual tradition, you will find different schools of thought. Some will say all Afrikan deities are manifestations of the primary creator deity, and some will contest that notion. I believe that the representation of the one idea gained more traction due to monotheistic religions invading Afrika. Sometimes both are true in which they emanate from the one, and they are separate beings; for this reason and others, Afrikan cannot adopt their practices to this category of polytheist.

Panentheism

Panentheism is the belief that the divine pervades and interpenetrates every part of the Universe and extends beyond time and space. The term was coined by the German philosopher Karl Krause in 1828 to distinguish the ideas of Georg Wilhelm Friedrich Hegel (1770–1831) and Friedrich Wilhelm Joseph Schelling (1775–1854) about the relation of God and the Universe from the supposed pantheism of Baruch Spinoza in panentheism; God is viewed as the soul of the Universe, the universal spirit present everywhere, which at the same time "transcends" all things created. While pantheism asserts that "all is God," panentheism claims that God is greater than the Universe.

Some versions of panentheism suggest that the Universe is nothing more than the manifestation of God. In addition, some forms indicate that the Universe is contained within God, like in the Kabbalah concept of tzimtzum.

Also, much Hindu thought and consequently Buddhist philosophy is highly characterized by panentheism and pantheism. The primary tradition on which Krause's concept was built seems to have been Neoplatonic philosophy and its successors in Western philosophy and Orthodox theology.

Panentheism Analysis

The main problem with the panentheism definitions that don't fit Afrikan spiritual culture is their separation of God and existence. Afrikan cultures do not believe that their creator deity pervades time and space. They don't think that God created the Universe, and he is separate from that creation. Their creator deity is time, space, and the Universe because of its existence. In Ghana, according to the Akan, individuals are made up of kra (soul), honhom (breath of Divine Life), sunsum (spirit), and mogya (blood). The kra, the life force, emanates from Nyame. The kra is the tiny bit of Nyame that lives in every person's honam. Given at birth, it is the spiritual component of our consciousness and influences all of our actions. On an individual basis, the sunsum is the basis of one's character and personality and originates from the father. It is a functionary of the kra in that when Nyame gives us our kra at birth; it is the sunsum that escorts the kra; on physical death, when the kra returns to Nyame, it is again accompanied by the sunsum.

According to the Ashanti and Akan, the Universe is endowed with sunsum. The Akan Universe is endowed with varying degrees of force or power. This force or power is called sunsum, also called "spirit." You probably guessed Nyame created sunsum and is sunsum, and when one dies in Akom tradition, the sunsum returns to its creator Nyame. The Zulu people also regard God as existence. In the book Conflicting Minds by Ngubane Jordan, he cites Zulu culture by saying, "Zulu speaking monarchies of antiquity believed that all things had their origin in UQOBO; everything in the cosmic order evolved from UQOBO. This UQOBO was primordial consciousness; it had no beginning and no end; it was the infinite total of the values of all things which together made the cosmic order". In other words, nothing is outside of this phenomenon because existence is the phenomenon.

Pantheism

Pantheism is the belief that reality is identical to divinity or that all-things compose an all-encompassing, immanent god. **Pantheist belief does not recognize a distinct personal anthropomorphic god and instead characterizes a broad range of doctrines differing in forms of relationships between reality and divinity. Pantheists are monists.**

Pantheism was popularized in Western culture as a theology and philosophy based on the work of the 17th-century philosopher Baruch Spinoza, particularly in his book *Ethics*, published in 1677. The term "pantheism" was coined by mathematician Joseph Raphson in 1697 and has since been used to describe the beliefs of various people and organizations.

Pantheism Analysis

This one is simple; pantheists don't believe in creator deities but recognize all nature as divine. Although Afrikan has this concept of nature being religious, there is always one entity that is hailed as the creator; even with a deified ancestor, there is a first ancestor, the one that should be revered, worshiped, and thanked. For this reason, pantheism cannot be a correct spiritual category for Afrikan people.

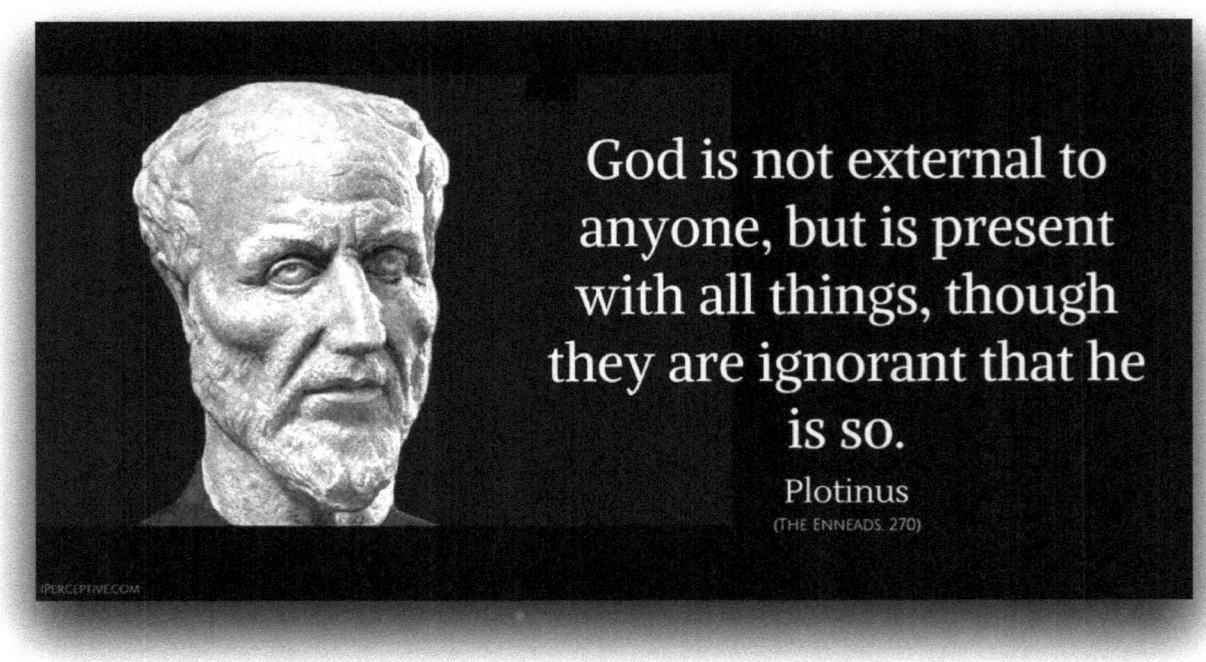

Neoplatonism

Neoplatonism is a term used to designate a strand of Platonic philosophy that began with Plotinus in the third century AD against the background of Hellenistic philosophy and religion. The term does not encapsulate a set of ideas as much as it encapsulates a chain of thinkers that began with Ammonius Saccas and his student Plotinus (c. 204/5–270 AD) and stretches to the sixth century AD. Even though Neoplatonism primarily circumscribes the thinkers who are now labeled Neoplatonists and not their ideas, some ideas are familiar to Neoplatonic systems, for example, the monistic view that all reality can be derived from a single principle, "the One." The term is a modern historiographical term, and the thinkers to whom it is now applied did not use it to describe themselves.

Neoplatonists believed human perfection and happiness were attainable in this world without awaiting an afterlife. Perfection and happiness, seen as synonymous, could be achieved through philosophical contemplation. After bodily death, the soul takes up a level in the afterlife corresponding with the level at which it lived during its earthly life. The Neoplatonists believed in the principle of reincarnation. Although the purest and holy souls would dwell in the highest regions, the impure soul would undergo purification before descending again, to be reincarnated into a new body, perhaps into animal form. Plotinus believed that a soul might be reincarnated into another human or even a different sort of animal.

Neoplatonism Analysis

Neoplatonists believed human perfection and happiness were attainable in this world without awaiting an afterlife. Perfection and happiness, seen as synonymous, could be achieved through philosophical contemplation. I shouldn't have to go any further, but I will. Afrikan spiritual traditions don't stress being perfect. They emphasize good character. The difference is that Afrikan deities don't make this claim and correct themselves all the time. Let's examine the Senegambian creator deity Roog. He is known as the source of all life, the point of departure and conclusion, he is both father and mother, but Roog is not to be prayed to directly.

Roog is also known not to get involved in the day-to-day affairs of man. There are no claims in Roog's literature that I can find of him being perfect. In fact, this narrative seems to be strictly an Abrahamic claim amongst their deities. In Roog's literature, there is a story of him reorganizing the Universe to cease a conflict. There was a conflict between animals, plants, and humans. Roog realized his mistake and reorganized the Universe to correct it. A God that restores himself? It sounds like a foreign concept to most, and it is because all you have heard is God is perfect, but we have just discussed how the Afrikan God is not.

Henotheism

Henotheism (from Greek ἑνός θεός *(henos theos)*, meaning 'one god') is the worship of a single god while not denying the existence or possible existence of other deities. Friedrich Schelling (1775–1854) coined the word, and Friedrich Welcker (1784– 1868) used it to depict primitive monotheism among ancient Greeks. The latter term is an extension of "henotheism," from καθ' ἕνα θεόν *(kath' hena theon)*, meaning 'one GGodat a time. Henotheism refers to a pluralistic theology wherein different deities are viewed to be of a unitary, equivalent divine essence. Another term related to henotheism is "equitheism," referring to the belief that all gods are equal. Further, henotheism does not exclude monism, nondualism, or dualism.

Henotheism

Henotheism Analysis

Henotheism is a passive-aggressive approach to understanding the spiritual world. They believe in worshiping one deity but don't deny the existence of other deities. Afrikan spirituality acknowledges the creator deity and celebrates other divinities. So much so that in many Afrikan traditions, the deities have their schools of learning. For example, Damballah may be the creator deity in Haitian Vodou, but Ezruli Danto has her songs, dances, colors, and mode of worship.

Monolatrism

Monolatrism is distinguished from **monotheism**, which asserts the existence of only one God, and **henotheism**, a religious system in which the believer worships one God without denying that others may worship different gods with equal validity.

Monolatrism Analysis

Monolatry would work for the Afrikan spiritual world if it weren't for the shrine component in Afrikan spirituality and its importance in worship. We worship deities at their shrines; we give offerings, chant to them, sing and dance. This is how we interact with them, but with our creator deities, that does not happen.

Why? You might ask, and it's because our creator deities don't have any shrines. Shrines are received by those you want to make that worship personnel, but how would you do that with a deity that represents all of life? One could argue that all of the Universe is one shrine to the creator deity. With this in mind, Monolatry cannot be accepted as the spiritual Framework for Afrikan people since the concept for this category worships deities on equal footing.

Kathenotheism

Kathenotheism is a term coined by the philologist Max Müller to mean worshipping one God at a time. It is closely related to henotheism, the worship of one God while not rejecting the existence of other gods. Müller coined the term about the Vedas, where he explained each deity is treated as supreme in turn.

Kathenotheism Analysis

The Kathenotheism one-at-a-time concept will not work for the Afrikan spiritual framework. Festivals are happening simultaneously in many traditional Afrikan systems across the continent in the same country. These festivals acknowledge different deities, but they are in the same pantheon. We also honor various deities within the same festival for other reasons.

Let's look at some Afrikan systems

Dogon

According to Dogon, the highest creator or sky god is Amma. Nommo was the first living creature created by the sky god Amma. Nommo can be a proper name for an individual or refer to the group of spirits as a whole. The Nommo are ancestral spirits sometimes referred to as deities. The word Nommos is derived from a Dogon word meaning "to make one drink," The Nommos are usually described as fish-like creatures. Folk art depictions of the Nommos show creatures with humanoid upper torsos, legs/feet, and a fish-like lower torso and tail. The Nommos are also referred to as "Masters of the Water," "the Monitors," and "the Teachers. Amma is the Dogon name for Amen. Amma is the intelligent consciousness behind all creation and the awareness within all beings. Amma is 'He Who Rests Upon Nothing.

There are many misconceptions about the Dogon spiritual tradition. This is mainly because the new age movement is high jacking their spirituality and fitting their stories to meet their beliefs. This mischaracterization of the Dogon's practices is shameful but let's clear up some misconceptions. The Dogon became famous when a French anthropologist named Marcel Griaule traveled to Mali and met with an elder named Ogotemmeii for 33 days. This elder told Marcel the ancient stories of the Dogon tradition. He also mentioned the star we know today as Sirius. He told Marcel that there was another start behind Sirius. How did he know? He knew because the Dogon had observed the stars' orbit cycle. This cycle takes 50 years. During this observation, they noticed that Sirius had companion stars. When one of the companion stars called Digitara was close to Sirius, it brightened, and when it was further away, it gave a sparkling effect. This suggested to the Dogon that other stars were in a cluster around Sirius A. This is how they knew about Sirius B before modern Astronomers. The Dogon has a game called Ein in which 12 pebbles and 12 holes were presented. The game is supposed to resemble their God, Amma, moving the stars in the sky. The Dogon has many symbols in their writing, like the one in this picture, which means a sign of the beginning God named Amma.

A Fat Roog

The creation myth of the Serer people is intricately linked to the first trees created on Planet Earth by Roog. Earth's formation began with a swamp. The Earth was not formed until long after the creation of the first three worlds: the waters of the underworld, the air, which included the higher world (i.e., the sun, the moon, and the stars), and Earth. Roog is the creator and fashioner of the Universe and everything in it. The creation is based on a mythical cosmic egg and the principles of chaos.

The Serer people believe in a supreme deity called Roog (or *Rog*) and sometimes referred to as *Roog Sene* ("Roog the Immensity" or "The Merciful God"). Serer tradition deals with various dimensions of life, death, space and time, ancestral spirit communications, and cosmology. There are also other lesser gods, goddesses, and supernatural spirits or genies (Pangool or N*guus),* such as the Fangool *Mendis* (or *Mindis*), a female protector of Fatick Region and the arm of the sea that bears her name; the God Tiurakh (var: *Thiorak* or *Tulrakh*) – God of wealth, and the God Takhar (var: *Taahkarr*) God of justice or vengeance. *Roog* is neither the devil nor a genie but the creator of creation.

Roog is the embodiment of both male and female to whom offerings are made at the foot of trees, such as the sacred baobab tree, the sea, the river, such as the holy River Sine, in people's own homes or community shrines, etc. Roog Sene is reachable perhaps to a lesser extent by the Serer high priests and priestesses (Saltigue), who have been initiated and possess the knowledge and power to organize their thoughts into a single cohesive unit. However, Roog is always on watch of its children and always available to them.

Children of the Forest

Africa's Mbuti Pygmies

KEVIN DUFFY

Mbuti

The most important God of the Bambuti pantheon is Khonvoum, a hunter deity who wields a bow made from two snakes that appear to humans as a rainbow. After sunset every day, Khonvoum gathers fragments of the stars and throws them into the sun to revitalize them for the next day. He occasionally contacts mortals through Gor (a thunder god who is also an elephant) or a chameleon (like the divine messenger used by Obatala of Yoruba mythology). Khonvoum created mankind from clay. Black people were made from black clay, white people came from white clay, and the Pygmies came from red clay. He also creates the animals that hunters need. These people are famous for equating their creator to the forest. The forest gives them food, clothing, and shelter. It protects them from storms and conceals them from attacks. It provides medical and is self-sustaining. Doesn't this sound like a deity to you?

Arebati is a lunar deity and Sky Father. In some sources, he was said to have created humanity from clay instead of Khonvoum.
Tore is a god of the forests who supply animals to hunters. He is also a thunder god who appears as a storm and hides in rainbows. Most importantly, Tore appears as a leopard in the initiation rites. The first Pygmies stole fire from Tore; he chased them but could not catch them, and when he returned home, his mother died. As punishment, he decreed that humans would also die, and he thus became the death god.

A Mbuti soul is called a megbe. When a man dies, his son places his mouth over his to draw part of the *megbe*. Another part inhabits the man's totem animal. If the son does not inhale the megbe or the totem animal is later killed, it may escape into the forest, where it becomes a semi-visible being called a Lodi and lives forever with others like it.

Ngoma

The word Ngoma is a bantu word with many meanings in the southern part of Afrika. You will find this word in isiZulu, Sesotho and, Xhosa languages. It refers to the spiritual practice of southern Afrikans. Traditionally, the more strongly held Zulu belief was in ancestor spirits (*amaThongo* or *amaDlozi*), who had the power to intervene in people's lives, for good or ill. This belief continues to be widespread among the modern Zulu population. Traditionally, the Zulu recognize several elements to be present in a human being: the physical body (*inyamayomzimba* or *umzimba*); the breath or life force (*umoya womphefumulo* or *umoya*); and the "shadow," prestige, or personality (*isithunzi*). Once the *umoya* leaves the body, the *isithunzi* may live on as an ancestral spirit (*idlozi*) only if certain conditions are met.

Behaving with **ubuntu**, or showing respect and generosity towards others, enhances one's moral standing or prestige in the community, one's *isithunzi*. By contrast, acting negatively towards others can reduce the *isithunzi*, and the isithunzi can fade away completely.

To appeal to the spirit world, a diviner (***sangoma***) must **invoke** the ancestors through divination processes to determine the problem. Then, a herbalist (***inyanga***) prepares a mixture (***muthi***) to be consumed to influence the ancestors. As such, diviners and herbalists play an essential part in the daily lives of the Zulu people. However, a distinction is made between white *muthi* (*umuthi omhlope*), which has positive effects, such as healing or the prevention or reversal of misfortune, and black *muthi* (*umuthi omnyama*), which can bring illness or death to others, or ill-gotten wealth to the user.

Mossi

The Mossi's account of their founding is handed down through the following myth: Over forty generations ago, a king named Naba Nedega had a daughter whom he would not allow to marry because she was a great warrior. Princess Nyennega took a horse and fled north into what is now Mossi country. She married a local man. Their son, named Ouedraogo (stallion), was sent back to his mother's homeland to be raised by his grandfather, Naba Nedega. When he grew up, he returned to the north with cavalry from his homeland and conquered his father's people, the Bisa.

The marriage of Ouedraogo and his troops with Bisa women produced the Mossi people. A statue of Princess Nyennega on horseback in Ouagadougou commemorates the story. University of Ouagadougou and Frederic titinga pacere, Augustine sonde coulibaly. The system of the Mossi has three main components. There is a belief in a powerful all-creator, Wende; fertility spirits of the rain and the Earth, which govern the soil and crops; and ancestors, who affect the lives of their descendants. Wennam- supreme creator associated with the sun. He is also called winde or naba zidiwinde. Some of his manifestations are Tenga Wende(female)Tido Wende, Siguiri Wende, ki Wende, saga Wende Holy land, and wend pous neba. Land of the priest and priestess.

Odinani/Omenala

Chukwu created the world and everything in it and is associated with all things on Earth. Chukwu is also a **solar deity**. To the ancient Igbo, the Cosmo is divided into four complex parts:

- Okike (Creation)

- Alusi or Arusi (Supernatural Forces or Deities)

- Mmuo (Spirit)

- Uwa (World)

The Igbo world is divided into several interconnected realms, principal among them being the realm of the living, the realm of the dead or the ancestors, and the realm of the unborn. Individuals who led an honorable life and received a proper burial proceeded to the ancestral domain to take their place among the ancestors ("*Ndichie*"), who were separate from the Alusi. From there, they kept a watchful eye on the clan and visited their loved ones among the living with blessings such as fertility, good health, longevity, and prosperity. In gratitude, the living offered sacrifices at the family hearth and sought counsel.

Ìṣẹ̀ṣe Làgbà

This word expresses what most people call Ifá. We don't call the whole tradition Ifá anymore because Ifá is the system of Ọ̀rúnmìlà and doesn't encompass an entire tradition of Òrìṣà practices from southwestern Nigeria. Each of these Òrìṣà has its own practice, literature, songs, dances, etc. The word Ìṣẹ̀ṣe is defined by Oloye(chief) Fama dictionary as primordial. Meaning beginning or in its earliest stages. It refers to the beginning of oneself and the beginning of the Yoruba ethnic group as a people. The Yoruba people acknowledge a creator deity called Olódùmarè, he is known by other names, but Olódùmarè is the most common one. Olódùmarè is everything from the air we breathe to the Àṣẹ in our bodies.

Olódùmarè is existence itself, and out of this existence came other deities in the Yoruba pantheon. The pantheon I'm referring to is called Irúnmọlẹ̀ and Òrìṣà, respectfully. These are the deities that humans appeal to for work to be done in their lives. Aspects of nature often represent them, but some are not represented by nature at all, and their phenomenon is not represented in an observable fashion. Each Òrìṣà has towns in which they originate, colors, literature, festivals, modes of worship, taboos, favorite offerings, poetry, and even days of worship. Each has its epistemology; if we compare it to schooling today, each would be a college-level course.

To learn the ways of just one of these Òrìṣà can take a lifetime and a half of studying. One nerve stops learning and perfecting one's craft of Òrìṣà. One that wants to symbolically marry the Òrìṣà and be a caretaker of its mysteries requires initiation. Although this is not necessary to be a worshipper, it is the next step up from devotee and a step in the direction of becoming a priest of said Òrìṣà. After one completes training, they are recognized by their trainer as a priest, conduct rituals on their own, and eventually train others.

Ki.môyo

I will now be introducing a new term to some. Still, this term will be what people like myself, Asar Imhotep, Kofi Piesie, and others are using to replace the word Afrikan spirituality. The word came out of the Kikongo language of the Congolese and was introduced to us by the late Dr. Fukiau. Ki.môyo heart refers to the vital part of the person. He further elaborates by saying, "The Bântu religion is not animism or animalism; neither are the Bântu animists nor animalists.

The Bântu people are "vitalists," this is accepting themselves as well as everything in the Universe as part of "N'kîngu a môyo," the principle of life in its wholeness. Their religion deals principally with Force and Vitality. A religion that does not believe in any physical being, but in "Ngolo ye môyo mu dingo-dingo" - Force and life through dingo-dingo, the natural way of life and change. This religion can be called "dynamo-vitalism," or Kimôyo. - Dr. Fukiau Digging Up the Past. Asar Imhotep has elaborated, stating it means force (energy or dynamism) and life (vitality). It is here that the Afrikan systems, in their aspect among the Bântu, find the roots of their dynamism in their wholeness. I will expand on this in my following text.

References

- Bowman, Marion (2004). "Chapter 1: Phenomenology, Fieldwork, and Folk Religion". In Sutcliffe, Steven. *Religion: empirical studies*. Ashgate Publishing, Ltd. pp. 3–4. ISBN 0-7546-4158-9.

- http://www.pewforum.org/2012/12/18/global-religious-landscape-exec/

- *Jewish Magic and Superstition: A Study in Folk Religion,* Joshua Trachtenberg, 1939, Forgotten Books, Preface, pg xxvii

- Cook, Chris (2009). *Spirituality and Psychiatry*. RCPsych Publications. p. 242. ISBN 978-1-904671-71-8.

- Brown, Peter Robert Lamont (2003). *The rise of Western Christendom.* Wiley-Blackwell, 2003. ISBN 0-631-22138-7, p. 341. Last accessed July 2009.

- Dubuisson, Daniel (2007). *The Western Construction of Religion: Myths, Knowledge, and Ideology.* Baltimore, Md.: Johns Hopkins University Press. ISBN 0801887569.

- *Rock, Stella (2007).* Popular religion in Russia. Routledge ISBN 0-415-31771-1, *p. 11. Last accessed July 2009.*

- Fred Reinhard Dallmayr, *Dialogue Among Civilizations: Some Exemplary Voices* (2004), p.22: Western civilization is also sometimes described as "Christian" or "Judaeo-Christian" civilization.

- http://www.themasonictrowel.com/Articles/Freemasonry/philosophy_files/the_volume_of_sacred_law.htm

- A Modern Hindu Monotheism: Indonesian Hindus as 'People of the Book.' The Journal of Hindu Studies, Oxford University Press, June McDaniel – 2013, doi:10.1093/jhs/ hit030

- Zoroastrian Studies: The Iranian Religion and Various Monographs, 1928 – Page 31, A. V. Williams Jackson – 2003

- Global Institutions of Religion: Ancient Movers, Modern Shakers – Page 88, Katherine Marshall – 2013

- Ethnic Groups of South Asia and the Pacific: An Encyclopedia – Page 348, James B. Minahan – 2012

- Introduction To Sikhism – Page 15, Gobind Singh Mansukhani – 1993

- The Popular Encyclopedia of World Religions – Page 95, Richard Wolff – 2007

- Focus: Arrogance and Greed, America's Cancer – Page 102, Jim Gray – 2012

- Monotheism 2012. Encyclopedia Britannica Online. Retrieved 12 January 2012, from http://www.britannica.com/EBchecked/topic/390101/monotheism

- Wikipedia

- https://en-academic.com/dic.nsf/enwiki/24440#cite_note-17

- Merriam-Webster Dictionary

- https://en.wikipedia.org/wiki/Nommo

- The Pale Fox by Griuale & Dieterlen (1986)

- https://en.wikipedia.org/wiki/Serer_creation_myth

- Children of the Forest: Africa's Mbuti Pygmies by Kevin Duffy

- The Peacemaker's Path: Multifaith Reflections to Deepen Your Spirituality by Jerry Zehr

- https://www.encyclopedia.com/social-sciences-and-law/anthropology-and archaeology/people/mossi

- https://www.wikiwand.com/en/Arusi

- Digging Up the Past: An Approach to Fundamental Education and Community Development (Case of Zaire) (Bilingual Education, Therapy, Revolutionary Theories) by Kia Bunseki Kimbwandende Fu-Kiau

www.ingramcontent.com/pod-product-compliance
Lightning Source LLC
Chambersburg PA
CBHW061418090426
42743CB00026B/3493